SECRETS OF
WALT DISNEY WORLD

SECRETS OF WALT DISNEY WORLD

**WEIRD and
WONDERFUL FACTS
about the
MOST MAGICAL
PLACE on EARTH**

DINAH WILLIAMS

STERLING CHILDREN'S BOOKS
New York

STERLING CHILDREN'S BOOKS
New York

An Imprint of Sterling Publishing
387 Park Avenue South
New York, NY 10016

Secrets of Walt Disney World is an independent publication and is not
associated in any way with the Walt Disney World® Resort, the Disney
Company, or any of its affiliates or subsidiaries.

The publisher has made every effort to ensure that the content of this
book was current at the time of publication. It is always best to confirm
information before making final travel plans as information is always
subject to change. The publisher cannot accept responsibility for any
consequences arising from the use of this book.

ISBN 978-1-4549-0814-2

Distributed in Canada by Sterling Publishing
c/o Canadian Manda Group, 165 Dufferin Street
Toronto, Ontario, Canada M6K 3H6
Distributed in the United Kingdom by GMC Distribution Services
Castle Place, 166 High Street, Lewes, East Sussex, England BN7 1XU
Distributed in Australia by Capricorn Link (Australia) Pty. Ltd.
P.O. Box 704, Windsor, NSW 2756, Australia

For information about custom editions, special sales, and premium and
corporate purchases, please contact Sterling Special Sales at
800-805-5489 or specialsales@sterlingpublishing.com.

Manufactured in China
Lot #:
2 4 6 8 10 9 7 5 3 1
08/13

www.sterlingpublishing.com/kids

CONTENTS

"All our dreams can come true, if we have the courage to pursue them."

—WALT DISNEY

INTRODUCTION

Since 1971, Walt Disney World has been a favorite destination for people of all ages. For the thousands of guests who visit one of the six parks each day, it's an enchanting place where imagination knows no bounds.

In *Secrets of Walt Disney World*, we've uncovered the little extras that make the park such a magical place. That way, when you visit, you can enjoy these special details. Or, if

you've already
visited, you
will learn more
about the things you
loved the most.

Throughout this book you'll find
tons of details, behind-the-scenes
tidbits, and fascinating facts about
the rides and attractions at Walt
Disney World. Read on to find out
how Walt Disney's incredible dream
continues to inspire and entertain
countless people every day.

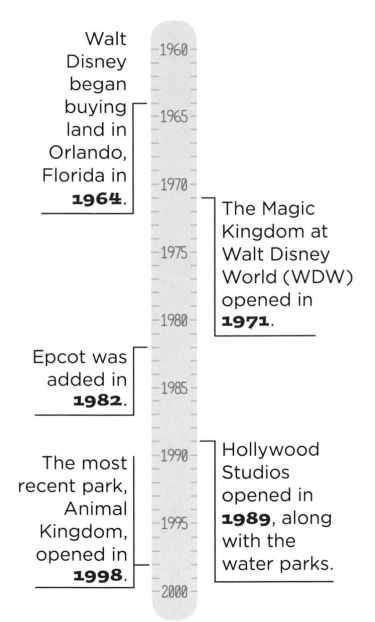

Walt Disney began buying land in Orlando, Florida in **1964**.

The Magic Kingdom at Walt Disney World (WDW) opened in **1971**.

Epcot was added in **1982**.

Hollywood Studios opened in **1989**, along with the water parks.

The most recent park, Animal Kingdom, opened in **1998**.

1960
1965
1970
1975
1980
1985
1990
1995
2000

Quick QUIZ

Walt Disney World Resort is huge. It's twice the size of Manhattan! How much of the 40 square miles has been set aside as a wilderness preserve?

a) ¼

b) ½

c) ⅓

d) ⅒

Answer: a

Walt Disney World gets millions of visitors each year. **Magic Kingdom** is the world's most popular park. **Epcot** and **Animal Kingdom** are the next most popular Disney parks. Since Walt Disney World opened in 1971, more than **500 million** people have visited. The busiest time to visit is between Christmas and New Year's.

Each year, **2.5 million** "mouse ears" hats are sold at Walt Disney World. Placed end to end, the hats would be about **175 miles** long.

Everyone who works at Walt Disney World is called a cast member. WDW has about **62,000** cast members. That is the most people employed in one place in the United States. Every single one must wear a **name tag**, including the horses that work there.

Lloyd

Visitors to Walt Disney World don't just enjoy the rides. They also enjoy the food! Each year they gobble or drink more than:

75 million
Cokes

★ ★ ★

300,000 pounds
of popcorn

★ ★ ★

10 million
hamburgers

★ ★ ★

6 million
hot dogs

★ ★ ★

9 million pounds
of French fries

13 million
bottles of water

★ ★ ★

1 million pounds
of watermelon

★ ★ ★

2.6 million
chocolate-covered
Mickey Mouse
ice cream bars

★ ★ ★

1.6 million
turkey drumsticks

Plus, WDW is one of the few
places on Earth outside of Hawaii
where you can get a Dole Whip.
Haven't had one? It's a delicious
pineapple soft serve. Yum!

Quick QUIZ

Below is a list of the tallest rides at WDW. Write numbers 1 through 5 to put them in order from tallest to smallest.

___ Cinderella Castle **(189 feet)**

___ Expedition Everest
(just under 200 feet)

___ Spaceship Earth **(183 feet)**

___ Space Mountain **(180 feet)**

___ The Twilight Zone Tower of Terror
(199 feet)

Answer: 3, 1, 4, 5, 2

How much laundry do cast members do on an average day at WDW? **285,000 pounds!** To do that yourself, you'd have to wash and dry one load of laundry every day for 52 years.

WDW has **1,500 Christmas trees**. To make them sparkle, WDW uses **700,000 LED lights**. If you were to string the bulbs end to end, the strand would stretch for **96 miles**!

LOST AND FOUND
Facts

WDW's Lost and Found gets an average of 210 pairs of sunglasses every day. Since the park opened in 1971, nearly 1.65 million pairs of sunglass have been found. Every year, the Lost and Found also collects about:

✔ **6,000** cell phones

✔ **18,000** hats

✔ **3,500** digital cameras

✔ **7,500** autograph books

Members of the design and development team for Disney are called **Imagineers**. The word is a combination of **"imagination"** and **"engineer."** They build all rides, resorts, parks— you name it! One of their new projects is Avatar Land, based on the *Avatar* movie. Construction is expected to begin in Animal Kingdom in 2013.

Walt Disney World has
1.8 million cast member
costumes in more than
2,500 different designs.
That's more
than **8 miles**
of clothes racks!
Each year, almost
13,000 new pieces
from more than **100**
designers are added.

There are **3** monorail lines: **Express**, **Resort**, and **Epcot**.

★ ★ ★

Each of the **12** trains is **203** feet long, has **6** cars, and can carry **364** passengers.

★ ★ ★

The **average speed** is **40** miles per hour.

★ ★ ★

The whole monorail system is **14.7** miles long.

The trains ride on a
track beam that is
only **26** inches wide.

★ ★ ★

Approximately
50 million people
travel on the
monorail annually.

★ ★ ★

Since 1971, the **total
miles driven** by
WDW monorail trains
would be equal to more
than **30** round trips
to the moon.

Disney has always had **pins of its characters** for sale. During the Millennium Celebration in 1999, people began **trading pins**. Today, thousands of guests trade pins with other guests and cast members from **around the world**.

Word Search

Find your favorite Disney characters
in the word search.

```
M N N L N K A H L A S D D P O
J V U I D H J L C N K O L A N
J A Z A W P D E A X N R A A M
R S O Y D U Y H D E V N R Z
T E Q K Z E V H D M D T O I Y
O E E F O E U Y A C Z I D M K
G F F F D P L U T O T D N Y R
Z Z Y G Y N O A C Y R P P T L
B M S B W M D F E E M P K G W
W S H J I A B Z B S X B Q Q L
O D K N I M Z E Y E K C I M U
B Y N S K D N N L A I R V A W
W I Y A R I E L F L N B O L Z
E G J D W A E W I P E Q B K W
V Q E D J J P O H B C P X K T
```

Aladdin   Donald
Ariel   Mickey
Belle   Minnie
Daisy   Pluto

Check the answer key on page 158
to see the completed word search.

The 2005 **Piece of History set** has some of the rarest pins. Each pin contains a tiny piece of an **actual Disney ride**. The first in the series was the **20,000 Leagues Under the Sea** pin. It contains a bit of the ride's submarine porthole in it.

There are 2,000 acres of grass at WDW. To keep it trimmed, cast members have to mow 450,000 miles each year. About how many times around the Earth's equator is 450,000 miles?

a) 5

b) 13

c) 18

d) 7

Answer: c

Audio-Animatronics are a form of robot created by Imagineers. They can **move and make noise** but cannot walk. The birds in the Enchanted Tiki Room at Disneyland in California are one of the first places the robots were used. Nowadays, Audio-Animatronics are used in every Disney park.

The **skin** of the human Audio-Animatronics is **made of rubber**. Every few years the **skin** must be replaced because it cracks.

MAGIC KINGDOM

The Magic Kingdom is open 365 days a year. The park has been closed only five times:

1 Hurricane Floyd

2 The September 11 attacks

3 Hurricane Frances

4 Hurricane Charley

5 Hurricane Wilma

Magic Kingdom is actually on the **second floor** of the park. The first floor is filled with **tunnels known as utilidors**. They were built first and then covered from dirt left over from building the Seven Seas Lagoon. In these utilidors, deliveries are made, cast members get ready, and garbage is taken away.

How many of California's Disneyland can fit into the huge parking lot of Magic Kingdom?

a) 2

b) 4

c) 5

d) 1

There are **five murals** in Cinderella Castle. They are made from more than **1 million** pieces of Italian glass tile in **500 colors**. There are also real silver and 14 karat gold pieces. The **15 foot by ten foot murals** took **22 months** to complete.

For *Beauty and the Beast* fans, **Gaston's Tavern** in New Fantasyland offers a sweet surprise. LeFou's Brew, named for Gaston's friend in the movie, is a **frozen apple juice drink** with a hint of marshmallow. It is topped with a passion fruit and mango foam. **Delicious!**

Cinderella Castle is only **189 feet tall,** but it looks much larger. One building trick they used was to make the bricks **smaller at the top** of the castle. This makes them look farther away.

★ ★ ★

Cinderella Castle is more than **100 feet taller** than Sleeping Beauty Castle at Disneyland.

★ ★ ★

The castle took **18 months** to build in 1971. It is strong enough to stand the **110 mile per hour winds** of a hurricane.

The moat around the castle is **6 feet deep** at the drawbridge. It is filled with more than **3 million** gallons of water.

★ ★ ★

There are **27 towers** on the castle and **13 gargoyles**.

★ ★ ★

During the holidays, the castle is covered with more than **200,000 Christmas lights**.

Behind stained glass windows in Cinderella's Castle lies a **secret apartment**. It was for Walt, but he died before he could use it. In 2006, it was turned into a **fancy place** for special WDW guests to stay. The floors contain **real gold tiles**. There is also a "magic mirror" that turns into a television. Guests are greeted with one of Cinderella's glass slippers!

When the park is closing at night, **something special** often happens. It's called the Kiss Goodnight. "When You Wish Upon a Star" starts playing throughout the park. Cinderella Castle lights up with **sparkles and colors**. Then, a recording of Roy O. Disney, Walt's brother, thanks everyone for coming.

In 2012, an attraction with **Casey Jr.**, the train from *Dumbo*, was opened at New Fantasyland. There are monkeys, elephants, giraffes, and camels in the four cars on the train. They **squirt water** at anyone who comes by the **Splash 'N' Soak Station**. This water playground is a great place to cool off on a hot day!

Quick QUIZ

The Prince Charming Regal Carrousel is the oldest ride at the park. It was built in 1917 by the Philadelphia Tobbogan Company. The carousel has 18 hand-painted scenes from *Cinderella* and 2,325 lights. Each of the 90 horses is one-of-a-kind. Cinderella's own horse is the one with _____.

a) a pumpkin on its head

b) glass slippers on its hooves

c) a gold ribbon on its tail

d) a long yellow mane

Answer: c

Guests of all ages enjoy **"it's a small world,"** a fun-filled boat ride through seven continents. The ride was originally made for the 1964/1965 World's Fair. It opened in WDW in 1971. More than **300 dolls** sing "It's a Small World (After All)" in **five different languages**. The two dolls from the United States are dressed as a cowboy and an Eskimo.

Mickey's PhilharMagic
is a 3D show on a
screen that
is **150 feet
long** and **28
feet high**! It
also has the largest cast
of Disney stars ever. The
film doesn't just look good.
It smells good too!
During the movie, scents
such as apple pie are
sprayed in the air!

On October 1, 1996, Walt Disney World turned 25 years old. To celebrate, Imagineers decorated the front of Cinderella Castle. They turned it into a giant 18-story birthday cake! More than 200 gallons of pink paint were used to make the castle look like it had been iced. The building was then decorated with:

26 candles,
each 20 to 40 feet tall

★ ★ ★

16 two-foot
candy stars

★ ★ ★

16 five-foot
candy bears

12 five-foot
gumdrops

★ ★ ★

4 six-foot stacks
of **Life Savers**

★ ★ ★

30 three-foot
lollipops

★ ★ ★

50 two-foot
gumballs

On January 31, 1998, all of
the decorations were taken down.
The castle was repainted to
its original colors.

Climb aboard **Walt Disney World Railroad** for a ride around the Magic Kingdom. The **steam-powered trains** are named Lily Belle, Roy O. Disney, Walter E. Disney, and Roger E. Broggie. The trains were built between 1917 and 1928. The 20-minute ride is enjoyed by **1.5 million people** each year.

Want to ride down Main Street in the style of the 1900s? Why not try a **horse-pulled trolley**? You could also ride an **omnibus**. The omnibus was modeled after a 1920 New York City **double-decker bus**.

Disney's Main Street **Electrical Parade** began in 1972. Since then, more than **100 million people** have seen it. The parade has about half a million lights powered by more than **500 batteries**. The dancers have **11,000 lights** on their costumes alone!

Word Search

Find your favorite Magic Kingdom attractions in the word search.

```
P T D D S F P U T Y V B D H R
H D N Y N C G Z S S L R S F O
I N A E Y A B V A X E M T X B
L A L L T Q L S D A Z Q T A B
H L E L J D P W M R D C R X N
A R R O T E E A O E M N G N W
R E U R Q C L A K R S Z M A H
M I T T B O K B B T R L G O N
A T N A N T H E O B I O W H F
G N E G W S E R N A G X M V Z
I O V U U F M H R T N J W O F
C R D Z S E Z O M H N L S D T
T F A A R T N W W O L I M D S
L L P P L O X C T E E E Z P D
X E S O M L L Q A P P V Y V M
```

Adventureland

Barnstormer

Dream-Along

Frontierland

Monorail

PhilharMagic

Tomorrowland

Trolley

Check the answer key on page 158 to see the completed word search.

Hop aboard one of the ten **27-foot-long boats** for the 9-minute Jungle Cruise. You'll travel at a speed of **3.2 feet per second**. The boats travel through three continents and **four rivers**: the Congo, the Nile, the Mekong, and the Amazon. Along the way you'll meet elephants, pythons, hippos, and a tribe of hungry headhunters.

The **Pirates of the Caribbean** ride begins with a 14-foot drop over a waterfall! You'll see **65 pirates** and villagers, 19 booming cannons, and 60 animals and birds. Keep an eye out for **Captain Jack Sparrow**! He appears at least three times during the ride.

What do **Walt Disney** and **Mark Twain** have in common? Walt Disney grew up in Marceline, Missouri. Mark Twain's novels took place in the make-believe town of St. Petersburg, Missouri. Walt created **Tom Sawyer Island** to bring the feeling of days gone by to WDW. To get to the island, guests take a ride on a raft. It's a great place to escape the crowds!

Since 1971, a cast of **18 Audio-Animatronic bears** have been performing the **Country Bear Jamboree**. It is the second-longest-running stage show at WDW, after the Carousel of Progress. The idea was originally created for a **Disney ski resort**, which was never built. The Disneyland version of the Jamboree closed in 2001.

Big Thunder Mountain Railroad took 15 years to plan. The **roller coaster** cost as much to build in 1979 as all of Disneyland did in 1955! The runaway train can reach **30 miles per hour**. The names of the six trains are: U. B. Bold, U. R. Daring, U. R. Courageous, I. M. Brave, I. B. Hearty, and I. M. Fearless.

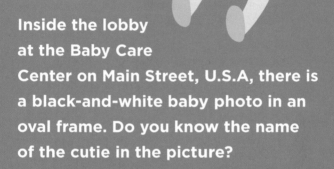

Quick QUIZ

Inside the lobby at the Baby Care Center on Main Street, U.S.A, there is a black-and-white baby photo in an oval frame. Do you know the name of the cutie in the picture?

a) Dumbo

b) Walt Disney

c) Mickey Mouse

d) Tarzan

Answer: b

Splash Mountain is the second most popular thrill ride after Space Mountain. The **log flume** follows Brer Rabbit into the briar patch. To get there, you barrel down a course almost half a mile long. On one **52-foot drop**, you reach speeds of **40 miles per hour**! Everyone sitting in the front row gets splashed by some of the **950,000 gallons** of water in the ride.

Liberty Square is a celebration of Colonial America. There are 13 lanterns for the original colonies hanging on the **Liberty Tree**. The original 13 state flags fly in a plaza. The **Liberty Bell** in the Square was made from the same mold as the actual Liberty Bell in Philadelphia.

Quick QUIZ

The Liberty Tree, a Southern Life Oak, is more than 150 years old. Since it was planted in Liberty Square, how many of its acorns have become young trees?

a) 300   **b)** 200

c) 500   **d)** 100

Answer: c

Do you want to meet **every single president** of the United States? Then visit the **Hall of Presidents**. It was built to look like Philadelphia's Independence Hall. President Obama's speech is not given by an actor—**it's the president himself**! It was recorded in the White House Map Room in 2009.

There are **999 ghosts** in the **Haunted Mansion**. They are hoping that you might become number 1,000! But it's not just the house that is haunted. In front of the house is a **black hearse** pulled by a ghost horse. Stand beside it and listen. You will hear the horse **whinny**!

Check out the **graveyard** at the Haunted Mansion. The **sayings on the stones** are about Imagineers who helped create the spooky attraction. For example, one reads "Master Gracey Laid To Rest. No Mourning Please At His Request. Farewell." This refers to **Yale Gracey**. He created the **dancing ghosts** in the ballroom.

What makes **Space Mountain** so scary isn't the **speed** (28 miles per hour) or the **length** (two and a half minutes). It's that most of the 4,000-foot-long ride takes place in the dark. The building that holds the ride is **183 feet tall** and **300 feet wide**. This makes it one of the biggest "mountains" in Florida.

Too young to drive a car? Not at Walt Disney World! Since 1971, kids have been jumping into the **sleek racecars** at Tomorrowland Speedway. You can travel up to **7 miles per hour** around a 2,000-foot track.

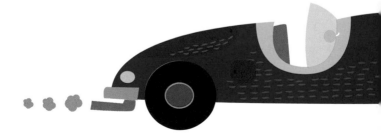

In the Africa scene of "it's a small world," look for Mickey in the **purple flowers** on a vine on the elephant's left side.

★ ★ ★

At the Haunted Mansion banquet, as the ghosts are dancing around, notice the **plate arrangement** on the table. It's a Hidden Mickey!

In the dark temple
on the Jungle Cruise, there
are **three plates**
on the steps among the
treasure that form your
favorite mouse.

* * *

During Wishes
Nighttime Spectacular,
look for a Hidden
Mickey **lit up on the
tallest tower** of
Cinderella Castle.

Wear a costume to go trick-or-treating at Mickey's Not-So-Scary Halloween Party. For almost 20 years, more than **215 tons of candy** is handed out each October. There are also more than **190** different **carved pumpkins** decorating Main Street.

Snow in Florida? It happens every night on Main Street in the days **leading up to Christmas**. So does Mickey's Once Upon A Christmastime Parade, with **Santa** and **Mrs. Claus**. People who buy tickets to Mickey's Very Merry Christmas Party can enjoy cookies and cocoa while they listen to **carolers**. They also enjoy special holiday **fireworks** and the park to themselves from 7:00 PM until midnight.

EPCOT CENTER CONSTRUCTION

BEGAN: October 1, 1979

COST: $1.4 billion

TIME TO COMPLETE: 3 years

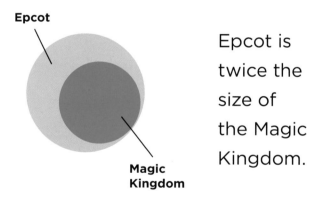

Epcot

Magic Kingdom

Epcot is twice the size of the Magic Kingdom.

VISITORS: In 2011, more than **10.5 million** people visited the park.

When it was being built, Epcot was the **largest construction project** in the world. More than **3,000** designers worked with **22** construction companies. They had more than **10,000** workers.

How many cubic feet of dirt was dug up to build Epcot?

a) 22 million   **b)** 13 million

c) 42 million   **d)** 54 million

Answer: d

Have you ever wanted to build your own roller coaster? **Sum of All Thrills** lets you! Using a touch screen, you decide the **height** and **speed** of the ride. You can also add features such as **dips** or **corkscrew turns**. A 4D robotic simulator then lets you experience what you've created!

Future World, Mission: SPACE recreates the experience of an **astronaut** on a mission to Mars. It took **650** Imagineers five years and **350,000** hours to create the ride.

The giant sphere took **26 months** to build. It weighs **16 million pounds**.

★ ★ ★

It measures **165 feet** wide and takes up **2.2 million cubic feet** of space.

★ ★ ★

Six legs hold this immense structure in place. They had to be driven **160 feet** into the ground to hold it steady.

The outer layer of
the **18-story-tall**
building is made up
of **11,324**
triangular panels.

★ ★ ★

Inside, a **13-minute**
ride traces history from
cavemen to the
present day.

★ ★ ★

If the sphere was
a golf ball, you'd
need a golfer
1.2 miles tall
to hit it.

Need a place to keep dry in the rain? Run under **Spaceship Earth**! Hidden behind the triangle tiles are a **series of gutters** that collect all of the rainwater. The water is sent down the legs of the sphere below Future World into the **World Showcase Lagoon**.

There is an **amazing water show** at the fountains in Innoventions Plaza every 15 minutes. There are **304 nozzles** that can shoot water **150 feet** in the air. If the nozzles all fired at once, there would be **2,000 gallons** of water in the air. At night, the water shows are lit with **1,068 colored lights**.

Test Track closed in April 2012 for a complete renovation. It reopened in December 2012 as Test Track Presented by Chevrolet. This ride enables guests to create their **dream vehicle**, then ride it at speeds of up to **65 miles per hour**. At the end of the ride, you can pose for pictures with your car, and even create a **TV commercial** for it!

The **Seas with Nemo & Friends's** 5.7-million-gallon saltwater tank is 203 feet wide and 27 feet deep. It is the **second-largest tank in the world**! More than **6,000** sea creatures in **60** varieties call it home. If you put the Spaceship Earth sphere completely in the tank, it wouldn't be big enough to touch the walls.

Looking for a great way to cool off? Visit Club Cool, which offers free samples of different Coca-Cola soft drinks from around the world. Currently there are eight flavors:

✓ **Krest Ginger Ale** from Mozambique

✓ **Fanta Kolita** from Costa Rica

✓ **Beverly** from Italy

✓ **Vegeta Beta** from Japan

✓ **Kinley Lemon** from Israel

✓ **Lift Apple** from Mexico

✓ **Mezzo Mix** from Germany

✓ **Smart Watermelon** from China (This appears to be many people's favorite!)

Word Search

Find your favorite Epcot attractions in the word search.

```
T  Y  V  J  U  I  M  E  E  D  E  K  V  N  G
S  L  I  D  F  C  M  A  T  B  Z  P  V  O  X
B  C  A  S  A  J  H  A  E  J  F  J  X  S  S
O  P  C  N  P  A  G  N  G  L  K  K  S  H  Z
Q  Q  A  H  X  D  K  C  F  E  S  D  R  T  K
O  D  S  A  O  L  L  B  V  P  W  T  K  D  D
A  O  C  M  D  R  O  T  K  N  F  O  R  O  Z
L  Z  Z  W  P  M  W  D  Z  T  Z  F  R  O  W
S  N  O  I  T  A  N  I  M  U  L  L  I  K  M
Y  N  A  M  R  E  G  A  M  B  M  U  S  E  S
V  B  I  I  Y  A  W  R  O  N  U  D  J  W  S
M  A  T  S  U  R  I  Z  A  F  W  C  U  R  R
S  N  O  I  T  N  E  V  O  N  N  I  E  D  G
L  U  W  Q  U  N  M  J  Y  I  P  W  L  D  P
U  D  X  B  O  O  R  Z  H  G  F  L  R  U  Q
```

Canada	Innoventions
Germany	Maelstrom
IllumiNations	Matsuriza
ImageWorks	Norway

Check the answer key on page 158
to see the completed word search.

In the String Greenhouse at Living with the Land, there is a one-of-a-kind **tomato tree**. In 16 months, it produced more than **32,000 tomatoes**. It won the Guinness World Record for the world's largest and most productive tomato plant. The fruits and vegetables grown at this pavilion are served at WDW restaurants.

Who created the beautiful **3,000-square-foot mosaics** in the walkway into The Land? A father and daughter-in-law team, Hanns and Monika Scharff. They spent three months installing **150,000 pieces** of marble, stone, glass, and gold in **131 colors**. They are the same designers of the murals in Cinderella Castle.

IllumiNations: Reflections of Earth is a 14-minute light and sound spectacular over the World Showcase Lagoon.

The show opened in **1999**. It was originally part of the **Walt Disney World Millennium Celebration**.

★ ★ ★

More than **1,100 fireworks** are used each night. They are shot from **34** different locations.

★ ★ ★

Four fountain barges pump **4,000 gallons** of water per minute.

A **150,000-pound** Flame
Barge has **37** nozzles.
They shoot flames **40** to
60 feet into the air.

★ ★ ★

The **28-foot-wide**
Earth Globe is wrapped
in **15,600** lights.

★ ★ ★

More than **26,000** feet
of lights are used to outline
the pavilions. That's almost
5 miles of lights!

The **World Showcase promenade** stretches 1.3 miles. Originally there were **nine countries**: Mexico, China, Germany, Italy, America, Japan, France, United Kingdom, and Canada. Morocco was added in 1984. Norway was added in 1988.

The **Temple of Heaven** in the China Pavilion is **acoustically perfect**. What does that mean? If you say something in the middle of the room, you can **hear your own voice echo**. The building is a one-half-scale replica, or copy, of the larger Temple of Heaven near Beijing.

The **Stave Church** in the Norway Pavilion was built in the style popular in the **Middle Ages**. The first was built in 1050! Currently only 28 still exist in Norway.

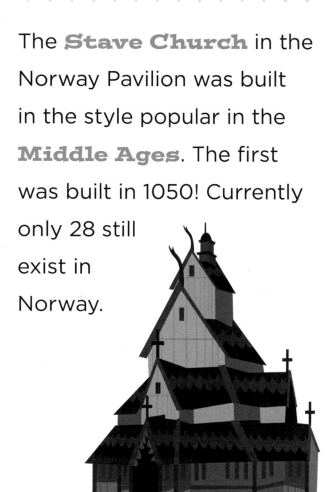

How many miles of bratwurst are served every 60 days at the Biergarten restaurant in the Germany Pavilion? Hint: It is the same length as a marathon.

a) 26.2   **b)** 14.5

c) 19.4   **d)** 22.7

Answer: a

The **83-foot-tall belltower** in the Italy Pavilion is modeled on the original in **St. Mark's Square in Venice**. How perfect is the imitation? The angel on top of the belltower is covered in **real gold leaf**. That's a lot of money spent on something you can barely see!

Why does the two-story **American Adventure** building **look so big**? It's another trick from the **Disney Imagineers**. A two-story building would not have been seen across World Showcase Lagoon. So the designers created a **5-story building** that looks like a two-story Colonial building.

If you look at the **tip board**
at Innoventions Plaza,
you'll notice the *O*
in Epcot is a globe. In it,
Australia is shaped
like a Mickey head!

★ ★ ★

Just as you are about
to crash through the
barrier wall in Future
World's Test Track, look
on the floor to your left.
The **coiled-up hoses**
form a Hidden Mickey.

At the beginning of the El Rio del Tiempo ride in the Mexico Pavilion, a **volcano** erupts every few minutes with a **puff of smoke** in the form of a Mickey head.

★ ★ ★

The sign outside the Sportsman Shoppe at United Kingdom pavilion has an **upside-down tennis racket** that forms Mickey's head. A **soccer ball** and a **rugby ball** form his ears.

If you are in the **Japan Pavilion**, listen for the booming sound of **Taiko**. This Japanese style of **drumming** is performed five times a day by a group called **Matsuriza**. They use drums that range from 6 inches to 6 feet high.

The **Morocco Pavilion** looks like three Moroccan cities: **Casablanca**, **Fez**, and **Marrakesh**. The King of Morocco sent his royal craftsman to do all of the tile work, carvings, and paintings. **Nine tons** of handmade, hand-cut tile were used in the **mosaics**.

The **Eiffel Tower** in the French Pavilion is one-tenth the size of the original. Disney Imagineers used Gustave Eiffel's **blueprints** to create the replica. The Tower in France is greenish, but the one at Disney is more of a brown color. This is not a mistake. Disney's Eiffel Tower is supposed to look like it did in the late 1800s.

Each year Epcot hosts the **Food & Wine Festival**. Over **45** days, more than **75** different international foods are served by **160 chefs**. This includes **1.2 million** hors d'oeuvres, **3,000** gallons of soup, and **100,000** miniature desserts.

The Epcot International Flower & Garden Festival occurs every spring. Cast members spend more than 24,000 hours preparing for the event. This includes:

Planting **500,000 plants**, **trees**, and **shrubs**

★ ★ ★

Tending to the **30 million flowers**

★ ★ ★

Releasing **1,000 native butterflies** in **10 species** in Bambi's Butterfly House

Planning **240** floating
mini-gardens in the
ponds between Future World
and World Showcase.

★ ★ ★

Displaying over
100 topiaries of
favorite Disney and
Pixar characters

★ ★ ★

Organizing the
Flower Power
Concert Series

Each year, performers in the American Gardens Theatre retell the **story of Christmas**. A 50-piece orchestra and a choir of 400 accompany them. There are more than 100 performances of the **Candlelight Processional** each year. The singers dressed in gold are high school choirs from more than **30 states**.

The **United Kingdom** has a long history. It was hard for Disney's Imagineers to **cram everything** into one pavilion. There are two castle replicas and the **crests** of the four major schools. There are also **eight different styles** of buildings: Victorian, London, Yorkshire Manor, Tudor, Georgian, Hyde Park, Regency, and Shakespearean cottage.

HOLLY-
WOOD
STUDIOS

HOLLYWOOD STUDIOS FACTS

SIZE: Nearly 135 acres

TIME TO BUILD: Nearly 3 years

COST: $500 million

- - - - - - - - - - - - - - - - - - - -

It features a replica of **Grauman's Chinese Theatre** in California. It also has handprints of famous people outside, just like the original.

Hollywood Studios
was originally going to be a
part of Epcot. However,
Disney Imagineers realized
everything **would not
fit** into one pavilion. That's
how it became its own park.
The **first movie** filmed
at Hollywood Studios was
Ernest Saves Christmas.

The Studios **do not have tunnels** underneath like the Magic Kingdom. However, Disney does provide a great way for cast members to get around: **bikes**. They are **shared** among the cast members.

The Twilight Zone Tower of Terror features an elevator ride that drops passengers over and over again. It is truly terrifying! Here are some more facts about one of the scariest rides at WDW:

The Tower of Terror at WDW is **199** feet high. The same ride is only **183** feet high at Disneyland.

★ ★ ★

The ride reaches its top speed of about **39 miles per hour** in **1.5 seconds**.

The **two** motors weigh **132,000** pounds each. They can move **10** tons at **15** times the speed of a regular elevator.

★ ★ ★

The Tower of Terror is made of **1,500** tons of steel, **145,800** cubic feet of concrete, and **27,000** roof tiles.

Quick QUIZ

The huge Sorcerer's Hat is a copy of the one Mickey Mouse wore in the 1940 classic film *Fantasia.* It weighs 150 tons and stands 122 feet tall. The hat was built to celebrate what would be Walt Disney's 100th birthday. Inside are computers with quizzes about Walt and his work. How many feet tall would Mickey have to be to wear this hat?

a) 280

b) 350

c) 400

d) 200

Answer: b

The **Indiana Jones Epic Stunt Spectacular** begins with Indiana Jones trying to outrun a massive **440-pound**, **12-foot-high ball**. This is just the start of an action-packed show. There are also 100-ton moving sets, **booby traps**, fight scenes, and explosions!

The Rock 'n' Roller Coaster is a super-fast ride featuring the rock group Aerosmith. Guests accompany the band as they race from a recording session to a concert. Here are some facts about this fun ride for music-lovers:

The "limo" cars go from **0 to 60** miles per hour in **2.8** seconds.

★ ★ ★

There are **two** rollover loops and one **corkscrew** turn.

Aerosmith music **blasts** out
of **125** speakers in each limo.

★ ★ ★

During the **3,403** feet
of track, you experience
a force of nearly **5Gs**. This
is more than the force of
the liftoff of the Space Shuttle,
which is only **3Gs**.

★ ★ ★

At **40** feet tall, the
guitar at the entrance has a
32-foot-long neck.
This is nearly **15** times
the length of the neck on
an average guitar.

Twenty minutes before the Indiana Jones show, cast members ask for **adult volunteers** to be in the next show. One of the people chosen is a **stuntman** who works for WDW. How can you spot him? He always wears a **Hawaiian shirt**!

The Star Wars movies were the inspiration for **Star Tours: The Adventure Continues**. C-3PO and R2-D2 are your droid pilots and there are **54 different ride combinations**. On one ride you may meet up with Darth Vader and Princess Leia, then end up on **Planet Naboo**. The next time you may start out with the Storm Troopers, meet with Yoda, and end up on the Death Star.

Want to become a Jedi? Sign up for Jedi Training Academy as soon as you get into the park. You'll get a **light saber** and brown robe to wear. During the training you'll learn **three things**: remember your training position, be mindful of your light saber, and no falling off the stage.

On **Streets of America**, look for the streetlight that has an **umbrella** attached to it. Grab the handle and step on the square in the cement underneath it. You will be rewarded with a refreshing surprise. **Here's a hint:** Have you ever seen *Singin' in the Rain* with Gene Kelly?

In the pre-show video at
Muppet*Vision 3D,
check out the **test pattern**
just after **Scooter** crosses
the screen for the second
time. It's a Mickey head!

★ ★ ★

In the Great Movie Ride,
in the second room of the
Wild West scene, look
up to the left. There is
a Mickey **silhouette**
on one of the second-floor
windows.

Visit the Stage One Company
Store outside Muppet*Vision
3D. Have a look at the **paint-splattered cabinet**
with the paint cans
at the top. You'll find
a Hidden Mickey in
green paint!

★ ★ ★

In Echo Lake,
the *O* in the **Radio Disney sign** has
a large Mickey
head inside.

Since 1997, Hollywood Studios has hosted **Star Wars weekends** four times a year. More than **60 characters** are there, representing all six of the Star Wars films: *Star Wars*, *The Empire Strikes Back*, *Return of the Jedi*, *The Phantom Menace*, *Attack of the Clones*, and *Revenge of the Sith*.

As you wait in line for **Toy Story Midway Mania!**, check out **Mr. Potato Head**. He is one of the most complex Audio-Animatronics ever made. The comedian **Don Rickles** provides his voice. He talks to guests, tells corny jokes, and sings. Sometimes he even removes one of his ears!

During the games each day, guests break more than **1 million virtual plates** using the shooters.

★ ★ ★

How many **toy soldiers** would you need to line the entire length of the track? A whopping **5,026**!

The ride is made so you
know how it feels to be
the **size of a toy**. People
who are five and a half
feet tall will feel
about **14 inches** tall.

★ ★ ★

The technology
used in the ride is
so complex
it cost an estimated
$80 million
to build.

Viewers watch **Lights, Motors, Action! Extreme Stunt Show** in a 5,000-seat stadium. This show features high-flying, **gravity-defying** automobile and motorcycle stunts as they are filmed for a movie. **Forty vehicles** spin, fly, and explode. Some of the fireballs explode 40 feet into the air!

Beauty and the Beast, Live on Stage is a 25-minute **Broadway-style musical**. It opened on November 22, 1991—the same day the film *Beauty and the Beast* opened in theaters. This was the **first time** that a movie and a show **based on a movie** opened on the same day.

This **25-minute nighttime extravaganza** is based on Mickey Mouse's dream about good and evil. Up to **9,000** people can watch the show at one time from the Hollywood Hills Amphitheater.

★ ★ ★

2,400 gallons of water are pumped **into the air** every minute.

The **Jafar cobra**
is **100** feet long
and **16** feet high.

★ ★ ★

The **Maleficent
dragon** is **40** feet tall
and weighs **32,000**
pounds. Its wings
are **50** feet wide.

★ ★ ★

The **80-foot** ship
from **Steamboat
Willie** carries **26** out
of the **50** performers
on it for the finale.

ANIMAL KINGDOM

Animal Kingdom has **1,700 animals** from **250 species** housed across **500 acres**. It is the largest Disney park.

In 1996, the first animals to arrive at the park were Miles and Zari, two young giraffes.

While planning Animal Kingdom, Imagineers traveled **500,000 miles** over **10 years**. That is the same distance as circling the Earth 20 times! The park opened on **Earth Day**, April 22, 1998. It cost nearly **$1 billion** to complete.

Did you ever notice the **dragon** in the middle of the Animal Kingdom logo? That was the symbol for the **Beastly Kingdom**. This park was going to explore **fantasy animals**, such as unicorns and dragons. It was planned but never built. **Camp Minnie-Mickey** is located in what was to be its place.

Finding
HIDDEN MICKEY

In the Maharajah Jungle Trek, look between the two tiger exhibits. On the right-hand wall past the archway you'll see a **mural of a tiger** in a river. Look closely at the water under the tiger. A **pattern of swirls** forms a Hidden Mickey.

★ ★ ★

If you could view Expedition Everest from above, you'd see that the **whole structure** is a huge Hidden Mickey.

On the **fire hydrant** across from Pizzafari restaurant, in front of the Island Mercantile shop, is a Hidden Mickey with **multicolored circles** for ears.

★ ★ ★

On the **mural** to the left of the Pocahontas stage, there is a Hidden Mickey **in the grass** between two trees, halfway up.

Quick QUIZ

Cast members prepare food for the animals that live at Animal Kingdom. How much food does it take every day to feed 1,000 animals? (A not-so-helpful hint: It is the same amount a person eats every 4.5 years.)

a) 1,000 pounds   **b)** 1 ton

c) 3 tons   **d)** 700 pounds

Answer: c

Dino-Sue in Dinoland U.S.A. is a copy of the **largest Tyrannosaurus Rex** skeleton ever found. She is 13 feet tall and 40 feet long. The original is **67 million years** old!

The **large cats**, which include tigers, cheetahs, and lions, are **trained** to work with their vets. They respond to **hand signals** or **voice commands**. The cats will open their mouths to have their teeth cleaned. They step on a scale to get weighed. They also **present their paws** to their doctors to be checked.

Approximately 1,500 two- to three-foot-long, hand-painted **wooden animal carvings** were created by **Bali craftsmen**. They can be seen on buildings throughout Animal Kingdom.

Quick QUIZ

In 2000, a black rhino calf was born at Animal Kingdom. The newborn weighed 80 pounds and was 28 inches long. Do you know how many black rhinos there are in the world?

a) 10,000 **b)** 580

c) 80 **d)** 4,800

Answer: d

At **Rafiki's Planet Watch**, there is an entire exhibit about **poop**. The lab at the Wildlife Tracking Station has tested thousands of samples of poop since Animal Kingdom opened. The tests provide information about the health of the animals. The best (or worst) part is when you get to hold **elephant poop**!

Word Search

The Flights of Wonder show includes many different types of birds, including the ones hidden in this word search.

```
H P W S O W J X S K L Y W L I
Z X F P V V A O J E R L W Z Y
Y K S A C Q B C A Y I O N X Z
M P H E L U I C A Y E R G I Q
L Q C W Z C L P M M C X Z J R
Q Y M Z Q D O I S E R I E M A
P Q A J B H Z N K W A H H W V
Y R X B J G Q A C D T N G F F
D H R X O G D Z H L Q K I Q E
K V C M U B I F P X L K U D M
C L J I C B Y M G C I F X W J
G G M L H P K E Z F U T F U M
P L G Y X N J V V N E F S C C
S N U U M T U A L H Y P B U U
A W E H C R A N E I B I S Z Y
```

Buzzard   Ibis
Crane   Macaw
Falcon   Owl
Hawk   Seriema

Check the answer key on page 158
to see the completed word search.

The Bat Cliffs house the **Rodrigues fruit bat**, one of the world's **rarest bats**. They are also the home of the **Malayan Flying Fox**, one of the world's largest bats. The Flying Fox's wings are six feet wide! Animal experts have taught the bats to fly inside for dinner when a **dog whistle** is blown.

FUN FACTS | The Terrific Tree of Life

Three Imagineers and **10 artists** worked for **18 months** to create the Tree of Life. The base of the tree is an upside-down oil rig.

★ ★ ★

The "tree" is one of the few fake plants among the **4 million living ones** in Animal Kingdom.

★ ★ ★

The tree is **145 feet high**, taller than a **14-story** building. The trunk is **50 feet** wide and **170 feet** across at the bottom.

Carved in the trunk
are **325 animals**,
from sea horses to
eagles to rhinos
and monkeys.

★ ★ ★

More than
102,000 leaves
in five shades of
green were attached
by hand to the tree's
8,000 branches.

Quick QUIZ

The Kilimanjaro Safaris Expedition features wildlife from Africa. Circle the animal you won't see at this attraction.

Antelope

Baboon

Black rhino

Cheetah

Crocodile

Elephant

Flamingo

Gazelle

Giraffe

Hippopotamus

Lion

Okapis

Ostrich

Penguin

Warthog

White rhino

Wildebeest

Zebra

Answer: Penguin

The **safari road** may seem **really old** and **bumpy** but that's on purpose. Imagineers matched the concrete to the **color of dirt**. Then they rolled tires through it and **tossed stones**, dirt, and twigs into it. That's the recipe for making a rarely used African road.

The Forbidden Mountain at Expedition Everest is almost **200 feet** high. It is the **tallest of 18 mountains** created by Imagineers.

★ ★ ★

The **34 people** on each railway car follow the twists and turns for nearly a mile, including an **80-foot drop**.

★ ★ ★

To recreate Mount Everest in Florida, more than **900 bamboo plants**, **10 species of trees**, and **110 species of shrubs** were planted.

More than **1,800 tons of steel** were used to build the mountain. An office building the same size would use **six times less** steel.

★ ★ ★

To cover the rocks and village, they used **2,000 gallons of stain and paint**.

Six baby elephants have been born at Animal Kingdom since its opening in 1998:

✔ **Tufani**, a male, born in 2003

✔ **Kianga**, a female, born in 2004

✔ **Nadirah**, a female, born in 2005

✔ **Tsavo**, a male, born in 2008

✔ **Luna**, a female, born in 2010

✔ **Jabali**, a male, born in 2011. He weighed 311 pounds at birth!

Hundreds of pieces of **real African artwork** dating back to **8500 BC** are on display in the Animal Kingdom Lodge. One of the coolest is the **Igbo Ijele mask**. This mask is 16 feet tall and 8 feet wide. Created by the Igbo people of Nigeria, this type of mask is **made to dance** by a man hidden inside. This happens every 10 to 25 years at important events and celebrations.

WATER
PARKS

There are **two** water parks at Walt Disney World. **Blizzard Beach** is a winter-themed wonderland. Here you can take the chairlift to the top of Mount Gushmore. **Typhoon Lagoon** has the world's largest wave pool. It has **2.75 million** gallons of water!

The wave pool at **Typhoon Lagoon** is twice the size of a football field. **Surfers love it!** Waves up to 6 feet high break every 90 seconds.

Are you afraid of sharks? If not, you can snorkel through a 360,000-gallon **saltwater tank** in Shark Reef at Typhoon Lagoon. It has stingrays, bonnethead sharks, and leopard sharks. It also has **4,000 tropical fish**.

An average of
2 million people
visit Typhoon Lagoon
each year, the
most of any water
park in the world!

★ ★ ★

Miss Tilly's
smokestack
erupts with a
**50-foot-high
geyser** every
half hour.

The Humunga Kowabunga
is a ride with three
enclosed "speed slide"
flumes. It sends you down
5 stories at a speed
of **30 miles per hour**.

★ ★ ★

In Hideaway Bay,
the Crush 'n' Gusher has
three water coasters
that pump **1,350 gallons**
of water per minute
to push you down drops
of up to **420 feet**!

Quick QUIZ

Ski Patrol Training Camp is a special area at Blizzard Beach for big kids. Which of the following is NOT a part of this attraction:

a) An iceberg obstacle course

b) A zip line over water

c) Inner-tube slides

d) A toboggan race down a mountain

Answer: d

▼▼▼▼▼▼▼▼▼▼▼▼▼

Castaway Creek is a 15-foot-wide, 2,100-foot-long river. It slowly flows through Typhoon Lagoon. While **drifting** on inner tubes, you pass through **gentle waterfalls**, lush rainforests, mist screens, and **Mount Mayday**. The whole journey takes 20 to 35 minutes.

Summit Plummet is the biggest attraction at Blizzard Beach. It is **120 feet tall** and reaches speeds of 60 miles per hour. It's the **second tallest** and fastest **free-fall slide** in the world—behind Beach Park in Brazil.

What's 90 feet tall and 250 feet long?

Slush Gusher! This snow-themed body slide reaches speeds up to **35 miles per hour**. Two places on the slide almost level off, but then drop back down again. This is the best place to catch air.

ANSWER KEY

PAGE 25

```
M N N L N K A H L A S D D P O
J V U I D H J L C N K O L A N
J A Z A W P D E A X N R A A M
R S O Y D U Y H D D E V N R Z
T E Q K Z E V H D M D T O I Y
O E E F O E U Y A C Z I D M K
G F F F D P L U T O T D N Y R
Z Z Y G Y N O A C Y R P P T L
B M S B W M D F E E M P K G W
W S H J I A B Z B S X B Q Q L
O D K N I M Z E Y E K C I M U
B Y N S K D N N L A I R V A W
W I Y A R I E L F L N B O L Z
E G J D W A E W I P E Q B K W
V Q E D J J P O H B C P X K T
```

PAGE 81

```
T Y V J U I M E E D E K V N G
S L I D F C M A T B Z P V O X
B C A S A J H A E J F J X S S
O P C N P A G N G L K K S H Z
Q Q A H X D K C F E S D R T K
O D S A O L L B V P W T K D D
A O C M D R O T K N F O R O Z
L Z Z W P M W D Z T Z F R O W
S N O I T A N I M U L L I K M
Y N A M R E G A M B M U S E S
V B I I Y A W R O N U D J W S
M A T S U R I Z A F W C U R R
S N O I T N E V O N N I E D G
L U W Q U N M J Y I P W L D P
U D X B O O R Z H G F L R U Q
```

PAGE 49

```
P T D D S F P U T Y V B D H R
H D N Y N C G Z S S L R S F O
I N A E Y A B V A X E M T X B
L A L L T Q L S D A Z Q T A B
H L E L J D P W M R D C R X N
A R R O T E E A O E M N G N W
R E U R Q C L A K R S Z M A H
M I T T B O K B B T R L G O N
G N A N T H E O B I O W H F
I O V U U F M H R T N J W O F
C R D Z S E Z O M H N L S D T
T F A A R T N W W O L I M D S
L L P P L O X C T E E E Z P D
X E S O M L L Q A P P V Y V M
```

PAGE 138

```
H P W S O W J X S K L Y W L I
Z X F P V V A O J E R L W Z Y
Y K S A C Q B C A Y I O N X Z
M P H E L U I C A Y E R G I Q
L Q C W Z C L P M M C X Z J R
Q Y M Z Q D O I S E R I E M A
P Q A J B H Z N K W A H H W V
Y R X B J G G Q A C D T N G F F
D H R X O G D Z H L Q K I Q E
K V C M U B I F P X L K U D M
C L J I C B Y M G C I F X W J
G G M L H P K E Z F U T F U M
P L G Y X N J V V N E F S C C
S N U U M T U A L H Y P B U U
A W E H C R A N E I B I S Z Y
```

We hope you've enjoyed this brief tour through the secrets and highlights of Walt Disney World. While we've packed the book with information, there is so much more for you to discover. So start exploring and compiling secrets of your own!

If you enjoyed *Secrets of Walt Disney World*, check out *Secrets of Disneyland*! It has lots of **little-known facts** about Disneyland, the very first Disney theme park.

SECRETS OF
DISNEYLAND®

WEIRD and WONDERFUL FACTS about
the HAPPIEST PLACE on EARTH